Whispers Etched in Stone

Elisa Morelli

WESTBOW
P R E S S®
A DIVISION OF THOMAS NELSON
& ZONDERVAN

WestBow Press books may be ordered through booksellers or by contacting:

WestBow Press
A Division of Thomas Nelson & Zondervan
1663 Liberty Drive
Bloomington, IN 47403
www.westbowpress.com
1 (866) 928-1240

ISBN: 978-1-9736-0850-9 (sc)
ISBN: 978-1-9736-0851-6 (e)

Library of Congress Control Number: 2017917765

Print information available on the last page.

WestBow Press rev. date: 11/29/2017

This book
is dedicated to my mother,
Mary Helen,
and her love of poetry.

Contents

BOOK II

BOOK III

Acknowledgements

I am grateful to my editor, Alan Highley, for helping with yet another book. He never seems to tire of the written word, and his editing gives a finishing touch to things. I am thankful for his encouragement, professionalism and friendship.

Also, a terrific addition to this book are the sketches of Miss Emilee Gallegos. Thank you, Emilee, for your thought provoking art. Your drawings have added so much to the black of the ink and the white of these pages.

BOOK I

The Building Stones

(Isaiah 60:15 -61:12)
Lift up the banner for the peoples!
Go through, prepare.
Build up, and
take out the stones.

How many stones do you have?
Just a pocketful.
But if I use one of them to stone you,
Then I have one less for the building.

Lean to Light the Wick

Lean to light the wick;
be able to pass the baton.

Teaching the next generation
what they will need to know.

And they
in turn
will pass it on
to the next generation.

A Proverb

Practice.
Practice does not make perfect;
It just makes things permanent.

We are not practicing for tomorrow.
We are living today!
What we live today will bring results we *will* see tomorrow.

This is the day. Let us rejoice and be glad.
Let us be glad that it is today
and rejoice when it's over!

Not a Problem?

Not a problem? Not a problem.
When something is said, and it doesn't
Pertain to you,
Then let it 'ping off' of you.
It obviously wasn't meant for you anyway.

Our House

Of God's landmark.
I can see the thistling,
pines and woods of a grey and yellow.

They whisper to me
as I pass.

Why the woods so entwined
with the smell of musk
and undertones of thistle?

While I wait for the
woods to make my home,
I will think of you

And then see the
new growth as wine
and things to come.

The Noon Day's Breeze

I have had the laughter,
but I know now,
once again
I will breathe.

To Be In Position

Am I missing the point?
There must be more to life
than just feeling good.

Than scheming and trying
to position myself
so that I am in the right place
at the right time.

An old adage, given by
some good humanist, no doubt: "But be
that which you find yourself."
And, be in position to give.

That's Why

Many people will ask me, they'll say,
"Do you believe that you're going to heaven?"
And I'll say, "Yes."

And many will then ask, "But *why* do you
Think you're going to heaven?"
And I reply, "Because I told God
That I trusted Him." That's why.

The Race

Go through: it is the only direction.
And get through. I will give you more courage
and more strength than you can actually muster.
It's like breaking bricks with your bare hands,
like finishing a race, or completing a hard task.

Currency of Heaven

Some people believe in 'Karma.'
But Karma
is a belief system which roots itself
in the thought that
what we do, what we produce
is basically good.
That somehow we can produce
something – on our own –
that is good enough, kind enough,
to produce something so good
that it will come back to us AS Good
or better than it left us.

The basic belief system of this
is falsehood. It is impossible
for a mere human being
to cause something to come back
to yourself,
whether good,
or evil.
Ecclesiastes was written
by the wisest individual who ever lived,
and he called such thought 'vanities.'

A Great Grief

When you remember
loved ones
that have gone to the grave,
at first
you are overwhelmed –
and consumed.

At first,
the grief is so overwhelming!
There is nothing you can do.
Your heart is so taken aback by the loss.
All you can do is grieve
and think of the great loss of losing that person.

But as the years progress,
you might see
that the reason for such a great grief
is really because of such a great love.

You were overwhelmed by the loss so much
because of the great love that you shared.
No longer to touch and to hold,
but held only in your memory forever.

What a great loss, yes.
but what a great love as well!

The Hands of Time

My mind wanders; it
drifts. I am taken back, but only for a moment
this time.

It is almost like grieving a lover: Oh, I wish myself
a way to turn back the hands of time! My mind waits, but I howl
and you are no more.

How *do* I find hope again in a new day?
I was so used to looking forward to seeing you. Then, you passed by
and you are no more.

I wish, I want. I am
here again, waiting for the train.
I hear the whistle.

And every muscle in my body remembers
the rumble of the last time you came my way. I live in dying glory,
and am alone again on this mountain.

Created Equal

If we are really "in Christ,"
we are given front row seats
at what He is doing.

Knowing God's ways
We envelope one another
Day after day.

Why did we see such a need
To capture one another?
Your life against mine.

Plow the field, mark the land.
Push the sun; I know
It will get hotter.

But I'm still standing.
Battered and bruised, but
Still standing.

A long line, time worn.
The pursuit of happiness only run
In life and liberty, we're satisfied.

Behold these truths to be self-evident,
That all men are created equal.
Endowed by their Creator.

Upon a Rock (Written in China)

Magnificent!
The gates that lead
to nowhere.

In time, they fade.
Purple hue,
rain and mist
give way.

Unchanging,
the gates that lead
to the rock.

More than the mighty,
in grandeur, they stand
upon a rock
whose Name is too high;
written in stone.

The stone
Which the builders rejected
Has become the cornerstone.

Face Reflects Face (China)

Grace and poor
cry out together for
   many to breathe.

Life has manifest
more than can be imagined
   in One life time.

Handsome in might
clothed with purity.
   grandeur it is not,
but grace upon grace.

In the face
of many waters
   reflection of water
casts forth dreams.

Dreams to see,
and hear,
   and comprehend.

With the heart
my soul will exult,
   and not full comprehend.

But I have known my King,
The One
   Who stands on high.

The Heads of State (China)

Purple and mind,
craft and such
   has set up an idol;
things too precious.
   Moreover, I have seen
a vain thing. Many will
come and see it and be glad
   at the rage of the storm.

Purple and wind,
some say the same.
   Awakened by light,
some say, "a terrible sight."
   Storm, a wind, a mind.

Many will come to the
brightness of your dawning.
Selah
   Neglect shall keep it astray.

Living in the Square (China)

Tiananmen Square

More power than a grievance,
and so many respired.
   "Tell the story again, daddy."

"Mustn't awaken the giant,"
   they said. "But many came
at the sound. Wounded
   and marred on the street."

"Those of heavy minds
   went their way
never to recover again."

   "But what about those
that went on to endure,
   daddy?"

"Their faces, bright as
the sun, shown forever."

The little one smiled.

Never Too Old

As we grow older, people become
too old to change. Do you believe that?
Just the fact that things grow older
should tell us that change NEVER stops.

I have heard people say that they are too old

to learn something new. That at a certain age,
and advanced in years, we lose our elasticity
to learn new things. This just isn't true.

It may take longer, but learning never ceases.
God designed us so that we will know Him.
He is the same yesterday, today, and forever.
Our minds do not cease working!

We do not have that luxury, we are not
the same yesterday, today, or forever.
We have the capacity to live and learn,
to give and take away from what we know.

The only time we stop learning is if a disease
takes over. We find ourselves without the ability
to 'wonder' and 'wander.' Someone else must
hold our hand and help us on our way,
because we have lost the ability to think and to reason;
to choose and to change.

We are made to hold God's hand – and maybe another's.
Otherwise, At that point we cease to have the stability
that we were given as children. It is a proven fact that we have
the new brain synapses formed every day.

We should adopt a new motto: Never too old to live, and
live as if you were dying. But don't live as if you were dead. A
grievance against living with only a part of what we know
and are? We are not merely bones, but people of possibilities.

The Dreamer's Remorse Responded

I gave you breath; I guess I have a right to ask.
Some people go on their whole lives
trying to 'get their own way.' Why is that?

Do they not see time for others as important?
That what we burden ourselves with
would be better left in the Arms of another?

What if there were only two people
In the world? White color people and chocolate colored?
Would we still find the same 'brands' to brand ourselves?
Or would we find a way of inventing a grasp of society
where we are not the center of our own attention?

That must be it! We are so self-centered that we have lost
the capacity to feel! We no longer see in vibrant colors, but only that
of a simple grey; where everything we touch should be the same.

'My mouth is wearied by my madness,' the Dreamer says.
"There's only room in this world for one, and I am it! You came in
and messed things up! How dare you! I was doing fine on my own."

But to My dismay, there has been a change 'in the brand' over the years,
and things have gotten out of hand. So, the Hand that made you
decided to say hello. Is that cool? (Author and Finisher.)

La Route de St. Jacques (Paris)

You wait in the crevices of time.
Not so long ago a beauty.
Your splendor, a city of love holds your key.

Your toil, characters. You hid.
A bulwark, an art. Who are you?
Amassed by graves; tender.

Still worn in sorrow,
your own, but time will heal.
Saint Jacques. (1856)

The City That Never Sleeps (Paris)

To sleep, to slumber;
The dizzying streets remind me.
Encamped with tourists.

Age and The Sun

I am not old,
but I definitely
have had a lot of
sun on my face.

The Thorn

A thorn,
a grievance, I know.
The thorn,
the beautiful thorn!
Priceless.

A work of affliction.
Some things are a work of fiction.
And others are not.

Change

When we start
doing something,
we usually
don't just do
everything
all at once.

But we might
get used to doing
one thing
and then
add to it.

We call it sequencing.
You or I
stepped up to
walk in
our own ways.
I'm including

myself in that.

It says,
be careful
not to bite
and devour
one another.

Just an insider's look.

I'm speaking
and saying something
out loud, to
convert myself.

The Freedom

Those that have the need,
respond to the words presented on the parchment.

The attachment read, "To those who have need of
something presented, please give way and allow 'this'
to mold and guide you. We call it the new freedom.
No need to apply; all are welcome."

We gave our hats to them. And they needed our coats.
So, we gave them our coats. And instead of the offered freedom,
we quickly saw that we needed MORE. More of this, that they
were handing out so freely.

They demanded that we come back for more, though we
weren't exactly sure what 'the more' was that they were selling,
I mean, handing out so freely. I was so quickly embroiled by the whole thing,
and didn't even really know it. I was hooked.

First, just my hat was needed. Then, when they asked for my coat as well,
I went along with it freely. My only complaint came when they asked for
the well, my freedom.

I, at first said, "No, I save things only for those that are
closest to me." But I was led to give away
my standing and freedom as well.

The Dawning (China)

Break,
  fast the dawning
of the new creation.
  Might and power
have not hold to keep
  it away.
Night has come
  but a new day is dawning;
Light and freedom
  cry together.

  "Barricade the door;
we will see who has might.
  I will barricade the
field; none shall enter."
  Old school.
Maybe One has already.

Lanterns (China)

Just on the other side of
   the river, I see a light.
Many lanterns set ablaze
   by One.

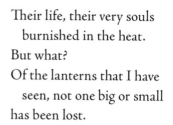

'Til it is dawn, they
   will stand watch.
Many come, many fall,
   but the lanterns –
pure in beauty –
   have taken a beating.

Their life, their very souls
   burnished in the heat.
But what?
Of the lanterns that I have
   seen, not one big or small
has been lost.

A Child's Reply (China)

"Keep it!" he cries.
Selfish ambition has given way.
   "I might as well keep it. It
is yours. I made it first
   for you."

   "I thought it would have a name,"
he recoils.
   "But yours is the only

name that it required."
    "I lost it; I'm sorry,"
he says, stumbling to
    make his way to the
old man holding the
    lamp.

    "But I gave it to you; it
will never be lost again."
    "Thank you." He smiled.
"I will never sleep again!"
    "Please, enter
and rest."
    "Thank you," came back
the reply.

The Great Ball (China)

I have read the whole thing;
I have known it since my birth.

There is only One:
Eternal, Triune, Creator, Divine God.

I have seen and my lips
Have uttered strange things.

Without my knowing it,
I have become a by-word.

Because of motion
I am hurled forward.

Like the great ball that I am on,
My mind has been made, renewed.

Silk Worm (China)

I stand in her gates
What a folly.
   Given to wanton
And pleasure,
   But no pleasure remains.

All there is
   Is an empty shell,
And empty casings
   Of what was.

So many,
   And yet none.

Many will come
   To the factory
But none will return
   There again.

The Regret (China)

The eldest sister
   thought forsaken.
As sheep running
   and never really
getting anywhere.

You have the beauty
   of nations,
yet one nation under God
   has deceived you

in some way.
  You hold,
but you do not.
  You perceive
but you regress,
  so many of you.

Money (China)

  Why such an honor
for one so fleeting?
  You make like
wings that do not light
  on you.

"More." But more
  will not be given; you
have drained the coffers.

Now rest. You will not
  come again.
Once it is gone,
  it's gone.

Just rest; you have
  been running to
catch up with your tail.
  do not expect a 'thank you;'
it will not come.

Speak My Mind (China)

"Maybe I should."
Too new to try it out.
I find every time I
open my mouth, the word
that comes out seems
the same: tail biter.

Finding the words is
just too hard; we have
so many things; much
too many to keep a count;
like a top up on its end.

I Rest (China)

Contented
   with what I have.
Not ready to gain more.
   Drained of all
my strength,
I stretch out.

I am glad to view
   the new day. Her
wrists are strong with
   bangles; jade and wine
have made me glad.
   So quick to choose,
but I wanted 'the more.'

And now,
   I sit down
to rest again.

Beijing and Time (China)

I *can't* stay first
on the stage,
    though I tasted the fun.
My nightmare
    became a reality.

So many came flooding in
    only to leave again; I
wish they could stay;
    my heart was wise – I
didn't give more than I said.

    So afraid; so marred,
but limping still.
    Grabbing at straws
and putting them back.

    I marry with the
foreign gods because
    I heard they were good.
I satisfied my
    curiosity. I found
all I needed was
    my own; but I did
not have my own.

    I wasted it on another.
Compassion I feigned
    and went another way.
I want and could not

have. All my racing
was against the wind
    only.

I had snow on the
New Year, but was
    surprised that,
satisfaction
    did not come.

Love Made Manifest (Britain)

(C.S. Lewis' House, The Kilns)

It wasn't a shrine; it was love made manifest.
So much time had passed,
the Lewis household.

Periwinkle blue,
on the bright umbrellas.
Living, sounds.
"What's life? My life." The discourse
goes on and on.
Love made manifest.

The gate, and what about the gate?
Humes, they swallow further than I'd like them.
As I said, the winter came all too soon.

Flush and swallow, they meet me here each morning,
To meet me in the hollow of the morning.
Grace is perfect.

Wine, comradery, and the witch
have taken up my mind.

"And forth come oft."

Wind and solitude,
and rest they will,
it's more than earth and sod.

You're almost there,
let me reach to touch you
once more.

The Little Yellow Bee (Britain)

(At The Kilns)

The little yellow bee; how small and sweet.
I firmly believe that as much as I can see,
You have no way of knowing
The call of the wild bird morning after morning.

The morning sky shall greet your day.

Miracles and Wishes (Britain)

(At The Kilns)

Drip the trees,
Mild with snow they lay.
A duck gaffing on the pond,
Perhaps the great willow, fortunate
To see its leaves;

Your wish to see the sentinel.
Crack of dawn by lights of day
Miracle awaits thee.
By lights of day, the sun in its waking.
A crane in its flight awakens my surprise.
Sweet oh sway, oh demon in flight,
As seen in the flight to ride to the dawn.

A Crest of Light (Britain)

(The Kilns)

Did you see it? That flash of light.
It crested through the sky;
I hardly awoke and
Burroughed in my pillow.
Its flashes awakened my sleep.

I, barely old enough to see
And moved by the sound.
Cradled by light,
Favorite morning break,
But now hewn by light.

The Trees (Britain)

(The Lake at The Kilns)

Along the mountain a ridge of columns grow.
Bridging deep and restful and full of hope.
What hollow sounds they leave;
Rippling wood and seedling vine.
Barely make me notice my footsteps are stopped.

Because first I see the tops of the trees;
The braided roof and charming!
The tall one is still there. Encumbered with grace,
Embraced by light.

Summertime Blessing (Britain)

(At The Kilns)

The weather-worn tie on the old gate;
Purpose and wonder were wrought through thee.
You made people smile, and generations have heard of
The fight.

The custom is to enter the fight,
And what generations used to see in bloom
Now they see in full color.

Where Love Abounds (Britain)

(At The Kilns)

Where talk of rights abounds
There is no grace.
But where love abounds,
There is freedom as well.

Fall Changes (Britain)

(The Kilns)

As leaves turn red
and then

smile toward the earth,
may you enjoy the
gentle Fall changes
of this new day.

Pilgrim

God is seeking all people.
And we hear His voice.
That's what lets us know that
We have a relationship with God.

He desires us.
It's undeserved. It is unmotivated love.
We could do nothing to hinder it,
Stop it, or to please Him more.
He gives us the gift of His love.
We may want to run
Or to make other people stumble,
And yet, in the midst of doing all these things
God comes and says, "I love you."

We are all Pilgrim.
It says, "All we like sheep have gone astray;
Each to his own way."

Lines Drawn in Pleasant Places

The lines are drawn in pleasant places.
This is poetic language: looking
At the face and seeing how time
Has changed someone's face.

How "the lines" that are drawn on the face
Are either lines of smiles, excitement;
Songs that have been sung, or lines
Of grief, and worn and riddled by time.

And this face is looking up at us
From a friend or relative that has just died.

You're not judging whether they are
"In heaven or hell," but whether during their life –
Looking back – the lines were
Drawn in pleasant places.

The Bad Day

Every insecurity that has ever lived
Inside my body is coming out.

My entire being is crying out
For release. I feel that I am nobody.

Who am I, thinking that
I can make a difference in my community!

And... how many
Of these thoughts are *really* true?

The Bicycle Spoke

The Bicycle spoke,
"And I believe
that when men
stop worrying
about *their* bicycles –

the size
of their bicycles –
and stop comparing
themselves,
and appreciate others
as human beings…,"

He trailed on:
"They are going to be
much
happier
people."

The Bicycle continued peddling,
"They are going to be
much happier,
and it will affect
the chain population."

"It will be powerful,
and our society
will look different."
(Based on I Corinthians 6:19)

"So,
implementing change
is possible,
and with perseverance
it will begin."
That's what the Bicycle said.

I Want

Take and take
have two daughters
   and I weary myself
with greed. I want
   and I take what is not
mine. I ask for those things
   which are wind,
and with that, like wings
   they leave me. I am
left with only the memory,
   but the memory does
not satisfy.

I want but cannot have.
I create, think and
   race after the wind
because I faint.

There is a rest
that is better. 'I will'
   is taken a back seat
to 'I have and will
   never more be.'
I am not; I seek.

Danger stands all
around. I have not
   the walls around to
encase me any longer.
   I feel like one who has
had their lovers escape
   me. I tried to hold them

in, but they did not
   see me anymore.

   Tired of chasing
the wind, I have had my
   fill. Dust remains.

Our Motivation

Our Neighbor: Do we want to beat him up
because we have anger in our hearts? Or

do we want to knock some sense into them
so that they can see they're going the wrong way?

There: two different motivations,
but the action might look exactly the same.

Harvest in Abundance

Let there be a harvest
of your heart!

That means that
whatever you sow,
that will you reap.

And that it would be
an amazing harvest.

And abundant,
and rich and full
from what you sow!

The Plumb Line

Think of a plumb line
as the chalk that is placed
on the ground
in one continuous line.
That line represents Truth,
the Person.

Anything that falls
to the ground
in a parallel line,
that doesn't follow
the plumb line,
is not Truth.

Some people
would like to believe
that a 'white lie' is
not a lie at all, but
a means to an end.

I'm here to say that
Truth is truth,
no matter how I 'lay it down.'

The Impersonal Pronoun

I.
You.
He, she, it.
Whatever you call It.

Only four fill the longing.

But I can't call You it.
"It" is just not fitting.

And if I think
"I" fits it at all,
Then I am unwise.
I is "unfitting."

Not for a King,
And certainly not
For the One who
Created.

On Manhood: Relating to 'Sisters'

Only One Wife, But Many Sisters

Though you will only have one wife,
you will have many "sisters"
with which to deal with in a lifetime.
There is the need for companionship
between men and women.
God made it that way for a purpose.

But so often the two don't come to
a true understanding of right relationships;
of interacting as God would have them do.
More often it's just a matter of finding a mate,
and having sex, and having babies.

But I believe God has a higher calling; one of design.
To make the two live in harmony with each other
without the overtones of war games –
power, possessions, etc. –
God has a purpose for both,
men and women.

BOOK II

With Military Poems

Brick Number 11

(The War)

Knee deep
in what seemed
  to be
the sands of time,
  I came to stand.

Whittled
as with a knife.
  Might, mantle;
holding together
  we stand.

Now. Ready
for action; no more
  armor to hold.
Laid waste.
  I am done.

God.
Stand.
  Stand firm
to the end.
  I am wasted.

The Battle

Too many to hold,
our countrymen.
  'Lost in a battle,

too heavy to stand.'
  Might and power is
seen to the right;
  harmony reigns.

  We wait, we travel.
Many are broken.
  I stand in the gate.
Horrible injustice
  and forgiveness
doesn't remain.
  Only the feeble hold to it.
I stand and rise!

Call to Greatness

  Forgotten nation;
is that your name?!
  Have you forgotten
how to rise.
  Maybe wanderers in
a land may be closer
  to the truth?
Thy mantle! Take it!
  You have forgotten
where thousands of years
  have brought you.
You are not your own,
  O great nation!
Guilt to rage them;
  set on fire.

Thank You to Service

Weak and wounded Warrior,
  You do not die in vain. Your blood
has shown crimson.

Weak and wounded warrior
  you are not alone;
there are many brothers around you, see?

Night has fallen; great darkness,
  but the sun will rise
to a much better warning: yours.

The Battlefield: Our Mind

The portals of our mind, the battlefield.
Do we neglect what we put into them?
Have we fed our minds with proper food,
Or only soul food?

What do we let our minds dwell on?
The answers will vary. Thoughts are given
because there is much that we dwell on.
Sports. Family Guy. Everybody hates Chris.
Pirates and warlocks. Supernatural.
Elaborate on one of these and there are
sure to be many answers,
given in detail.

We think we can plainly see and hear,
and touch and experience these things.
But to describe God's love?
What would be so vibrant a conversation?

Or to love God and neighbor,
would the answer be quite so clear?
And love God with all your heart, soul,
mind and strength without religion.

Our mind. Our mind. Guard it,
see what goes into it.

What gets past your portals?

Greatly Loved

I am reminded that I am 'a being'
and I am greatly loved.

I am not 'a doing.' I am more
than the sum
    of what I do and can produce.
I am a being.

A Word on Grief

Some say grief
        is
an unnecessary evil.
        I disagree.

I used to
gripe to
and about other
people.
But no more.

Their hurt caused enough
to feel with them
this season.

Things Out of My Control

My life is turned upside down!
What is my response?
Well, when I accepted the fact
that Jesus Christ, the living God
is a part of my life, then I acknowledged
that my life was not my own.

I gave up my rights:
rights to be comfortable,
of being in charge.
I no longer have the right to be
frustrated. Because frustration means
that I am still in control.

My lack of understanding
sometimes drains me of my feelings of joy.
I didn't say that it drained me of my joy, because
knowing God is deeper than
any feeling could ever be
inside my heart.

The Winds and The Waves

My heart is turning slowly toward You.
I can feel the breeze and
The water isn't so hard to get into now.

My fears are calming.
My aloneness Is the one thing I can count on
To be stable in my life. So many things have changed.

Changes while I was not looking! Please, give me
Signs of Your love and of Your compassion in my life.
All I see is what is around me.

My heart is continually overwhelmed
By the grief that pervades my soul. Once
As happy and free as a bird, I now lay awake.
And where did the time go?

Still not stable enough; my heart 'teeters' inside me.
I make mistakes
About what day it is, and how will I make it
From 'here and there.'

There is a hole I know only You can fill, and my heart
Has begun to cry out. Finally, my head is lifted
Above the waves
And I can see in all directions.

My eyes have been weary of searching
For my love, and
I can no longer hold him,
Or his hand;
Or revel in his love!
But I am convinced that I will see him again
Above the winds and the waves
In the land of the living.

No more dyin' there, and it is always day.

For a time I was silenced, my heart was made hard,
And my thoughts turned inward. But now, slowly,

My hands shoot up towards the skies and declare,
"Tu est mon Père!" ("You are my Father!")

I will wait for Your goodness.

The Potter, The Clay

Melt me. Mold me.
Fill me. Use me.

How can the clay say to the potter,
"You don't know me, or what you are doing!"

Even so, I say…. I am undone.

The B-I-B-L-E Without Religion

We outstretched our arms
To things that don't last,
but the First is still first
and will be there until the last.

The Truth still sits,
And will always be
Set above all,
Just wait and see.

A quick look at the B-I-B-L-E
as the age-old song,
I'm standing in the library
thinking about the old song.

The B-I-B-L-E is true
I might make mistakes
but the B-I-B-L-E is true all the time.

The B-I-B-L-E, the number one seller
doesn't ask forgiveness of you,
such a delicate subject
because religion overstepped
its boundaries and claimed to
always be true.

No other book claims that place
to sell more copies.

Outsells any cover,
and stays at 'the top of the charts'
when authors are placed
on the shelf.

If you go to the B-I-B-L-E,
you will embark on
an adventure; a journey.

The B-I-B-L-E cannot be figured out,
and yet simple enough a child can follow.
It is in our hands, or
in our hearts and transcends time.
Loved by people over the years
opened to a passage *and* always
something there: in your time of
need, in your joy, even in
your daily living.

People will disappoint, but
the B-I-B-L-E will stick with you.
And when you have
the pressures, you can
find something there that will
change your life in a positive way,
if you put it into practice

day after day after day.

The B-I-B-L-E?
Yes, that's the book for me.
I stand alone on the word of God:
The B-I-B-L-E!

My Own Way

I am convinced
In my heart that You are out to get me.
I've had that thought on and off
For a long time.

I am convinced
That if I move the wrong direction,
Or say something wrong, You
Are right there ready to condemn me
Or take away everything You have promised.

I am convinced
That You don't want me to have good gifts,
But rather, You want to be able to take things.

No wonder so many people have a hard time.
I have a hard time accepting
Your love.

And this is our work: that we believe in You
And that we believe in the work of the cross and
believe in all that You have for us.

Lord, right now, I ask You to make me.
Not to man's ways and to his will,
But bring me to You, the lover of my soul.

You have taken me through very tough times,
Not around, but through.
And have taken my pain. Thank You.
You really are my anthem.

Life for Good

What remains
forever in my life is
that action which
did not originate with me.

To Commemorate

(9-11)

We call it Patriot Day.
Is that because
people fell from a building
descending up
in a cloud of smoke?

Or because people perished
for being infidels? For being
judged by those who
consider themselves to be
of a higher calling.

Though they don't practice it,
they hold others to judgment.
Why does that sound familiar?
Merely "hearers of the Word and
not doers."

What makes us different
than the ones who destroyed our
Hallowed shores?
The blood of
The Patriot was shed many years ago.

We make our claim that He loves us,
then we are called to love and not judge.
More can be done
in His name than by all the
force in the world.

People will be wise to remember 9-11
as the day when the world stopped
and watched the 'wisdom' of man
burst onto the scene to take care of
the troubles in the life of sin.

Our lack of morals and character
put on the chopping block by Islamist
extremists. They used the verse that says
if you would rightly divide the word of Alnah
then you would not be judged.

As we commemorate,
let us therefore, press on
to know God. He seals our fate.
And our lives are in Him.

Gracious and merciful, God,
rich in lovingkindness, help us to love.
"Love others as I have loved you."

The True Man

God
desires truth
in the inner man.

And until we 'reposition'
our thoughts,
and say what God says is true,
then we are still living
in a state of confusion
and wrong standing with God.
We are His workmanship.
Ever-present and Omniscient.
Is there ever a point
when God says
that He is done making us!?

If we believe this, then
we have somehow given ourselves
over to a stale imitation
of something else,
and we are no longer
walking in the Truth.

The Line

Let the breeze
Blow away the chaff.
Let my heart be filled
With Your peace.

And may the power

Of Your might
be shown today.

You have tried my mind
And made me to want You.
You have shown Your great mercy
To those who walked in darkness.

Please give Your power
And Your grace for what's ahead.
And make my way straight.
Help me to hold the line.

The Conqueror

My life
Is a living testimony
to the faith.
We have this treasure
in earthen vessels.
Purge me with hyssop,
and I will be clean.
Wash me, and I will be
whiter than snow.
(Psalms 51:7)

I died and my life
is hidden
with Christ in God.
(Colossians 3:3)

I am rejected and accused
by my thinking,
I feel like a wanderer

in a lonely land. But You,
do not leave me — ever.
And Your mercies are new
every morning.

Today/Tomorrow

I wait, but not for today.
I have put all my hope in tomorrow,
    looking forward to seeing you again.

    Don't miss the moment.
But what about today?
    How can I be missing
out on today?

    I hear you say, "Come out
and play; don't wait
    and put your sights
on tomorrow!"

    Tomorrow is faint
and is a rambler,
    promises many things
but seems to never deliver.

    But I, I have the power
to deliver. I am today.
    Don't miss the moment.

    "A whisper and then a silence,"
the poet said. "Today" has said the same
    and made her call: "If you are wise,
you will look to today

and stop counting tomorrow."

Your words are for afar off day,
but that day never comes; it is
    always just a dream. Live in today.

I cannot say you will
not be disappointed today,
    but I *do* know you will be attracted
if you slow your pace
    and walk a while.

Clouds

The wind was set there for you to enjoy;
not to race after
    and see if you could overtake it.
Rest awhile and see if you can count
    how many flowers came out
to say hi to you today.

I bet you cannot count the hands
that raced forth to enjoy the day.
    They opened just for you!

The Face

I thought you were like me.
A smile
    And then a silence.
I am alone again,
    But this time, I will live again.
The lines are drawn
    In pleasant places.

The Old and The Young

It is lovely here.
The time passes slowly. It should not be made fun of;
    Why would you hold it
Out at arms length
    And say, "I will see you tomorrow!"
Isn't that a funny thing!

Retirement

Maybe this will help me smile at the sun.
It has been a long while
    Since I have looked up
And watched you dance, my friend.
    I became "too old" to see your eyes.

The Snowfall

I was touched
by the snow yesterday.

It caught my attention
  And I waited.

I opened my mouth
to
  catch
some
  on
my
  tongue.

Some Sports Poems

The Total Sum

When we look at our life,
how do we 'tally' everything up?
  If we are American,
it goes something like this:

If my job is successful,
And if I have friends,
  and I like my football team,
then I'm successful.

But that didn't answer the question, "When we look
at our life." That gave us a bunch of snapshots
  that didn't answer the question of 'we,'
and the measure of our life.

If we are only the total sum
of what we *did,* then the answer
   about job and friends
would be relevant.

Determined Action

Some people refer to Life as 'the game.' Okay,
so what team are *you* on? Which league?
   Do you have any opposition? Do you have teammates?

If life is a game, then isn't there a struggle? And
who is your team captain?
   Depending on how you answer those questions
will determine how we 'play' the "game of life."

We are not to play as if we don't have an opponent; beating the air.
How we decide who is the opponent will determine our action.
   We don't *really* determine our 'enemy;' it's already there.

The enemies are those things that we deem important.
What I mean is,
   until we stop, look and listen, we haven't entered into 'play.'
There has to be determined action before play.

Are you standing on the sidelines, watching someone else?
   Then you haven't entered the game.
Or are you one of the screaming fans? That's great,
   if it's not your turn to play.

Many a people lose 'the game' because they've
   been settling themselves on the sidelines. But once you know
that it's *normal* to have opposition, then you will have fully

entered the game, and have determined
   what sort of action is necessary.

Getting into the Scrum

   I want to tell you a story.
Our sons played on a rugby team.
   They would practice
four to five times a week,
   Then have a game.

   A scrum was formed: the sum
total exertion of an entire part
   formed as an enclave - to
come against the opposition.
   The force of the two teams meeting
caused quite a lot of injuries.

   As parents do, we would watch.
And in that whole season, there wasn't once when
   either someone wasn't carried off the field,
dislocated some part of their body,
   or broke something. You knew
there was a struggle.

   But being together, and
struggling towards a cause
   can produce injuries. But
that's how you know
   you've been in the scrum.

If you're not getting into the struggle,
   then why so much practice?

What Circumstances Dictate

When I see only my circumstances,
I am looking at something spiritually
Upside down, or not right-side up.

Promises. A place where I can
Hang my beliefs, like you would
Hang a coat or a hat.

Another use for the word hang
In that context would be to 'hang' my beliefs,
To forget them.

To allow my situation to rule. But God
Wants to rule in my life; He wants to
Be the center – not the circumstance.

What God says is true, not what circumstances dictate.
The truth of the matter is the fact, let every man
Be found a liar and God be found true.

Well, I say, let every circumstance – if need be –
Be found a liar and God be true! God, help me to see
The circumstance I am currently in from Your perspective.

Help me to lean on the power of Your love and Your ability,
Not my own. And help me to see what You see here, right now.

In Life With Teens

They are multiplying:
Friends and 'friends,'
TV games and computers.

The Miner: that one person who has found gold.
He chisels out the rock. You can see pockets of
refined gold, just running through the miner's veins.

Now is not the time to sleep.
"When the teens get older, life will slow down."
And if I sit back and not watch the signs,
I might find myself in a 'heap' of trouble.

The mine fields: standing in one spot,
surveying every piece of earth before I move.
Sifting through dirt, or on your knees
at the place where you realize
there are mines all around, on every side.

I pray over them. They're critical at these ages.
I mean, they're at these critical ages.
Their hearts are still tender,
but the influences coming in on them...
they are within inches of their lives.

Raising teens is like that: on your knees
looking for mine fields you may have overlooked.
The urgency grows as they gain in age.

Sometimes teens choose friends you
wish they'd leave. Their eyes toward these friends
are good, and they really like being around them.

You frantically find yourself down on your knees
to look for 'land mines.' And every waking moment
is like that sometimes.

But what does the miner do? That person who found gold?
He brought out mountains of gold from his pockets, "It's a process."

"God, please don't let them

get run over by a car."

"Lord, help them
to make right choices."

"Keep their minds pure."

"Help my heart to keep You first,
and not my children first."

"Let them know Your love for them."

Are We in the Habit

Are we in the habit of resolving conflict,
of covering people,
and so fulfill the law of Christ.

Or would we rather have a dung heap,
to see their mistakes and make them pay
to resolve the conflict; exposed to others.

We are to cover one another,
and so fulfill the law of Christ.

Or we may have two 'dung heaps:'
the person's situation and
our actions. Guilty.

We may smear it about some,
making it harder to clean up.
And smellier because it has been
examined and moved around.

Or, we would be able to save ourselves
and others in the 'clean-up,'

if we see the mistakes of others
as only things between them and God.

The Temptation: The Hard Times

"Lead us not into temptation."
Jesus' words.

I believe *temptation* can also be to not feel.
Being tempted to not go through the tough times.

Oh, we don't have to go through the challenges. We can
get out of it. But isn't that *also* a temptation?

It says Jesus endured the cross;
despising the shame.

He didn't choose the easy way out. He didn't choose to live
outside something real. I believe the cross was real.

There is a statement: "Pain brings joy." If that's true,
then we are doing a disservice to ourselves and others if
we keep ourselves from pain.

If we persevere through the pain, then on the other side,
we will understand, and it can encourage someone else's life.

You will have the stability to lift someone's hands.
Jesus said, "I call you friends."

He invites us to follow Him. And a part of following is enduring.
Though we may not like it, it's a part of the journey.
Persevere temptation. No temptation has overtaken us,
but that which is common to man.

The Parchment

The dry and dusty paper, His hands on mine.
He drew back the pages, and
opened the words anew.

Whew…
Aren't you glad
that Christ is King
and not you?

A Realization

You are not the Divine;
you don't become God,
  but God becomes real to you
as you follow.

You just forgot how to follow.
We are given front row seats
  to see what God is doing.

We become yoked with Him,
and it is possible as we follow
  we continually become
living sacrifices.

The Calling

(Paraphrased) "Enter through the narrow gate. For the gate is wide
and the way is broad that leads to destruction, and there are many
who enter through it. For the gate is small and the way is narrow
that leads to life, and there are few who find it." (Matthew 7:13-14)

Do you ever feel like you are being swallowed alive by circumstance?
Jonah's whale has been sent your way and you are the next in line.

Do you ever feel like you are wandering in the wilderness
and are trying to find a way to live?
Like everything that could go wrong has just done that?

Yet it is written that the Eternal Triune Creator
will not give us more than we can handle.
That's what it says.

You and I cannot get away from our calling.
We can run from it, yet it is still set there inside of us.
We in earnest can be learning what that calling means.

We stand on the shoulders of others,
and ours is to see what God will do through us.
No easy road, or at least that's what I've been told.

But still, wouldn't it be nice if we could stop our lives,
leave the wilderness and the whale,
and get our lives going?

What We Live

We live in a culture and society,
computerized or otherwise,
that no longer lives in one world.

We live in many 'altered states' of being.
And not one of those 'worlds' belongs solely
to one kingdom or the other.

And those lines are being blurred so much
that some people are pushing back the boundaries
for themselves.

What was the first and foremost command?
To go, and "To love the Lord, your God,"
and be a house of prayer.

We gave away the biggest battle fields
and didn't even know it.
Coffee, anyone?

If God Be King

We want to know the truth, so we ask questions.
What does God say about our mind?
Well, the first thing was that we needed to guard it.

He said that if we let a little leaven in,
that we would have mixture.
That if we did only what our culture did,
we didn't answer the question correctly.

What does God say about our minds?
That we love God with our heart and soul,
and love our neighbor as ourselves?

That's a misquote of what He said.
He said, (paraphrased) "You shall love the Lord,
your God, with all your heart, soul, mind, and strength. And
love your neighbor as yourself."

The detail that is most left out
Is mentioned in 3 of the 4 gospels. The greatest command,
repeated for those who have ears to hear,
is the detail that is most left out.

"Rabbi, what is the greatest commandment?"
Jesus answered, "The foremost is, "Hear, O Israel!

The Lord our God is one Lord."
There is no other greater.
(Paraphrased from Mark 12:27-31)

But If There is More

If you want to get 'beat up' to feel better,
go to the nearest religious person;–
the modern-day Pharisee and scribe.
But if there is more...

Follow the norms of society,
whatever they may be: have a dog, a rodent.
But if there is more...

Soul searching, not brow beating.
What you read is just one person crying out,
"If this is all there is, then we're not doing such a bad job."

But if there is more...

The One Who Speaks (China)

No man in life
or in darkness
can overcome the
One named upon the stone.

Last and least they come.
Riding with a name
written in blood.

Coming to the fiery
furnaces, but not

burned; but bright
  with bronze as their
portion.

  Hail! Those who conquer
No more forgotten
  in the city;
the city of strength.

  Coat and hat remain.
But see, names written
  in brightness.
All will see and some
  will hail
in like kind,
  the One.

  Making and made
In the likeness of
  flesh,
crowned with
  righteousness and
truth.

A band on His leg.
  A burnished piece
Made strong.
  Why come? Why look?
The King has already
  made Himself strong.

  There is none who can
Stand BEFORE THAT GREAT
      AND TERRIBLE DAY!
Just the One.

The One
Standing mighty,
   mighty in strength,
the robe of His glory
   shall stand
whiter than snow.

   Bronze in nature,
grown and grafted
   together with song.
Angels in Chorus,
   echoes remaining.

   "I see Him who was before
all things and standing,
   a candle."

   Nothing adds or takes
away from it, and
   it goes to do that which
it has accomplished.
   Mighty in wind,
sound in doctrine.

   The fate of a nation
now stands.
   A sigh,
of resignate
   and soulful purpose,
lie together,
   humbled
in the state.

The Emotions

My heart is in Your hands.
Why should I worry?
I tell myself, "You can't be frustrated.
Only receive and trust."

Three emotions:
Throw out frustration and
keep the other two?
You are good.

Keep the one and it hinders our ability.
I look up and see You there,
waiting for me.
You are silent.

I tremble
because I have
nowhere else to go.

My heart and my flesh may fail me,
but You are
the anchor to my heart,
and the strength of my flesh.

We Call, He Answers

Not the answer to our prayers,
Or in the boasting of the answer.
One is empty and vain,
and chasing after wind. Vanities of vanities.

God gives us the desires of our heart.

It is He who wills and works
His good pleasure
In us.

In and through us is His direction
for blessing the world today.
Ours is to lay aside the hindrances.

Without the help of the Lord,
there would be no boasting;
only death
and chasing after the wind.

On Contentment

Marbled
by anxiety,
by weight,

though nothing
rises in the road
to meet me,

and though
my way seems
vague.

The perch is empty.

I am learning
to listen
to You,

for You have the words of Life, so they say.

The Complaint

Some things seem so simple.
We hear something said, and someone else
doesn't hear the same way we heard.

And we wonder, "Why is it so difficult for
them to understand? I understood it perfectly."
But I could ask the same thing of you.

When it comes to things I see,
in the same way,
how can you not know
that God has revealed Himself to you?

Easter Message

It says, "God laid on Him the iniquities of us all."
Remember the game: slap each other as hard as you can?
The first person to give up, the other person wins.

And no matter how hard we press
And hit and slap and have our own ideals,
In one day, God won against the one who held it all.

So either waking or sleeping,
We are Christ's.
No more hitting.

Nails 4 U No. 1

The sign at the nail salon,
"Nails 4 U, Number One."
Do you care?

Well, if you are at all concerned,
then it's a pretty good sign.

But where are you going: Heaven or hell?
Some people have no interest
in that sign at all.

Pentecost Sunday

Today
In the church calendar
Is Pentecost Sunday.

There is
A world wide
Movement of prayer.

We pray to
Enthrone You
Before the entire world.

Holy Spirit, come,
Transform our hearts.

God All Around

God,
I am right where You want me:
Without a prayer
And in need of Your grace.
Move Your hand on my behalf.

My Double Mind

(This is for Youth)

Realizing that
what I would like to do
and what I do
are two different things,

I envision myself
calling
or writing the public,
making a plug
or being helpful.

Yet I feel that
my contribution
is not so significant.
That what I do
doesn't matter.

But the truth is
always different for me:
I think one thing
and the reality is
so much more encouraging.

I believe
that one thing
is a failure,
and it turns out
to make the biggest success.
It happens
over and over.

I want to meditate
and dream about the things
that *You* have put in my hand to do.
That n*ot for myself a success*
but because that one thing
You have put in my hand to do
will make all the difference.

You Saw and Rescued Me

I have wanted so many things,
and You have always given me life.
When I was drowning, You came and,
in Your timing You rescued me.

I was going down for the last time,
but You rescued me. I was lost and all alone,
with no one to save me, and You saw
and rescued me; pulled me out of the clay.

God is greatly to be feared,
And to be held in reverence
by all those around Him.

The Cry of the Poor (??)

I think
it's much easier
to 'weep
with those that weep'
than to 'rejoice
with those that rejoice.'
But
we are called to do both.

Childhood Dreams

My childhood dreams.
Remembered,
Forgotten.
What a painful time.
I am Your servant.

I can't feel You,
But I know You're near.
Your presence
Surrounds me.

I am like one
Who hides their face
until the pressure's over.
God, be my Stronghold, and
not my childhood dreams.

Light Tomorrow

Tomorrow is a new day,
full of hopes and promises.
Tomorrow I'll find You there,
when it is called today.
The mountains are high
surrounding Jerusalem.
The ones hiding in darkness
have seen a great light.
But there is none besides You.

It's been said before, many times
in different ways, but the fact is
that Your love upholds me constantly.
Let Your light shine through me, and
give me favor.

A Community of Strength

What do people build on inside of you?
Is it ego? Or is there something more to life?

Are we just the product of our environment?!
It's all about building; having a net of people.
A community that makes a net that won't break.

And that is held together, and will encourage
one another daily. Or are we given to
stroking ourselves by our selfishness?

I know the preparation is the most
important thing I do today.
Though the flesh is dead and in sin,

the spirit is made alive! And
God brings our spirits to life.

God brings our spirits to life,
then our natural bodies catch up.
And then our natural bodies
catch up to that which God is doing.

I realize the preparation is the most
important thing I do today.
I am agitated and engrossed in living,
but it is Your Spirit, God, brought to life in me.

And then the rest of the time *God*
gives life to our mortal bodies, the community.
It is God's will to work His good pleasure in us.

Prepared

God planned for this day
long before you were born.

God prepared what was to happen
long before it ever happened.

And we've been given a measure,
so love your neighbor, and do good
to those that despitefully use you.

We've always just said,
"Do unto others as you would
have them do to you."

But render to Him glory,
whatever is in your hands to do.

(Jeremiah 1:12) Then the Lord said to me,
"You have seen well, for I am
watching over My word to perform it."

That which looks small,
and that which looks insignificant,
are those things
that God uses to change the world.

Motivation

It's not by might, or motivation.
And it's not by power,
but it is mighty to the pulling down
of strongholds.

When we are motivated,
our motivation should be
just to know Him, and to love Him.
He is the One who said He is God
and we can worship Him.

We are changed daily
into that which we worship.
Whether God or the devil,
we become like the one
that we seek after.

We can't seem to have the
motivation to seek the Living God.
We can know that He is,
and that He loves us.

We were never the ones
seeking Him anyway.

He has always been the One seeking us.
We are the recipients
of His love.

Unmotivated Love

Let the bones which Thou hast broken rejoice!
I can't seem to do anything but stand.
I know that I have found Your pleasure,
when I have done all to stand.
Stand, therefore, as it's been written.

Sometimes, in the stillness,
in the quiet place
is where I find
those things
that will last for a lifetime.
My best work.

These aren't necessarily
times when I am
trying to do something.
But those moments when
I have stood against everything,
and in doing the things that are
In my hand to do.

And walking towards
the One that loves me,
because He is purely
motivated out of love.
I don't want to do anything,
I don't want to get
anything out of it.

That is called unmotivated Love.

I just want to be with my Love!
I want to be with Him.
He is the One who is
seeking my life;
to will and to work
His good pleasure in me.
All I have to do is respond
and to stand; unmotivated.

The Pinterest Point

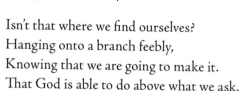

How about the age old Pinterest
Of the Cat.
From the branch
And the caption reads,
"Hang in there, baby!"

Isn't that where we find ourselves?
Hanging onto a branch feebly,
Knowing that we are going to make it.
That God is able to do above what we ask.

He will make His plans clear;
All we need to do is trust Him,
Know that He has our best in mind.
Staying away from 'the doubting wall.'
Hanging in there, away from the cliffs of insanity!

We believe that He has lost His motivation towards us.
There are too many scriptures that say that
His heart is toward us, He loves us. We can go
Back to John 3:16 if we have to:

"For God so loved the world that He gave
His only begotten Son, that whosoever..."

Don't go over the cliffs of doubt.
Instead, hold onto those things which you know to do.
Be faithful with the little things. God will be there.
He's not slow, as some count slowness. He is right on time.
And He will be there and make us strong
in our weakness.
He will do it! It is a fact.

Don't give in, don't give up. Hang in there, baby!

Liability

How good is God's timing?
I mean, how great is His liability?
Do I believe in His promises?
What He has promised, will He do?

How we answer those questions
is a matter of how we live out our lives.

And if I live treating God
as if He's always late, never on time;
that His promises are under review,
what does that say about my faith?
(And I am talking directly to myself.)

When I come up against these emotions
of complaining, and telling God
that I don't believe His timing is perfect,
over and over again, I need to
discipline myself. Here's
where liability begins.

The Parable of the Sower

There is something that I wanted to remember,
But I didn't write it down.
So now I sit in earnest
Trying to remember what it was
That was so important to me.

The Bible

A 'wee book.' It is very small,
   with very few words,
but given to
   [explode],
to impact
   our world.

Peek a Boo

   Don't hide.
He wants you to bring yourself
   to Him. (Hebrews 4:13)
"When you come to Me,
   don't hide or compare."

   Psalms 51, God says, "I want to
know what's inside of you." We say,
   "I want to show You, God."
We can't change ourselves. It's like
   a door turning on its hinge.

Dependence

Does what you say and do matter?
It depends on Whose you are
   or what you are connected to in life.

Many people in the U.S. can't stand the sound of silence.
They have dependence on some music playing in the background
   or something visual going on at all times.

They are 'connected' to these things. But,
if you are not *more* connected to the Living God –
   spending time with Him, getting to know
what He wants in the earth at this time in history –
   what you say and do will have little effect.

It will be
a 'clanging gong' or a shiny cymbal; very pretty
   but hollow sounding.

The Sound of Love Calling

(John 3:16)

Not all
who call on the name of the Lord...
is an empty statement
when made
by those,
that have
no idea
Who the God of *change* is.

There is nothing new

under the sun,
that's what they say.

Many will come
to eat at table,
we
will be surprised
to see all the faces
that we once condemned as lost.

But it was *my* own soul
that was so lost
and so blinded
by what I saw.
Jesus,
now,
I lay it
all aside.

I Know that You alone
hold the keys
to sin and death.
And that You alone
are humble,
and I am not.

You are the Head
of all things,
and though I tried
to 'begin' the work,
the 'end' things
were wrong.
I'm sorry.

Please fulfill the desires
of my heart.
Make me hear
the Sound of Love calling.

BOOK III

A Place of Belief

I don't know if anything is true anymore
Except that the blood of the spotless Lamb cleanses me
From shame and guilt.

I don't know anything anymore,
But God raised Jesus from the dead
So that I could walk in newness of life.

You, Lord, have ordered rest and complete healing
For those that did not have strength.
In the midst of turmoil there is the eye of the storm
Where everything is calm.

It is from that place
That I rest in Your promises.
Thank You for having care for me.

Life Without Fig Leaves

There is a reason why He is called The Victor and not victim!
Nailed to the tree, the new Adam turned over a new leaf, as it were.
Resurrected. His victory wood remains forever.

We choose how we will live our lives.
That's exciting! We don't have to hide or sow fig leaves.
God has made a way.

It's amazing.
He is the victor, there is no one higher.
The tree that lifted Him gave us the choice.
Turn over a new leaf, or not.

The Driving Force

Make me more like You:
a servant, a lover of people.
I want to see Your kingdom come, and yet
I'm weak and poor and don't always see it.

I can be quite jealous and need attention,
yet You are the One I really need;
to catch Your attention.

I want my own way
instead of seeing the needs of others.
I want to push my own way
and be seen or noticed.

Let my selfish ambition
take a back seat.
And let me sit for once
and watch others' 'rise to the occasion.'

There will always be
'Better ways of dealing with situations,'
and I think I have all the answers.
But just for once,
let me sit back and not be noticed.

A Word to the Weary

(Psalms 84:5-7)
(Isaiah 40:28-29, 30-31)

Open your life to serve
and to sow.
The Lord knows
those in the house get tired.
Don't give up. Having done everything,
to stand.

A Leader's Prayer

I fail more often than I win.
I blow opportunities more often
than I give encouragement to others.

I stink at relationships right now.
I have little to offer in the way of leadership.
I back paddle most of the time
and forget what's important.

I have failed. But
in the midst of my failure,
You encourage me.

Your voice says, "I am here. I did not leave you
or move." O God, give me encouragement
to see You moving in my life.
I need courage.

Little Put Downs

We feel like a kid,
asking for You to touch this area.
We pray specifically for the area
of 'little put downs.'

I might be stretching it, Lord, but
Father, Lord Jesus, Holy Spirit,
to repent for 'little put downs.'

The mocking of another person
behind their back or to their face.
I need Your power, Your strength,
to defeat the enemy in the way.

On Humility

The first step to revival
Is humility.

"God says a certain action is sin."
We disagree.
We justify ourselves.

We point to our friends
who did 'it.'

We point to
other people who are
'much less spiritual then
we are.'

Everyone in society
accepts this conduct, and

"how unfair of God to criticize it."

We can either justify what God says,
or we justify ourselves.
Humility.

The Great Commission

"All authority
On earth is given to Me," says the Lord.
And Jesus came and spoke to them,
saying, "All authority
has been given to Me in heaven and on earth.

Go therefore and make disciples
of all the nations,
baptizing them
in the name of the Father and of the Son
and of the Holy Spirit,
teaching them to observe all things
that I have commanded you;
and lo, I am with you always,
even to the end of the age."
(Matthew 28)

The Image Maker

I will not give up the fight.
I will turn myself
like a flint toward the goal.

You are my goal, You are
my stronghold.
I will rush to You

when times are hard.

I will not turn away
from Your love.
I want something to give
that is right from Your throne, God.

Whether there are
tens or thousands listening,
that we will have a word
from You to refresh their souls.

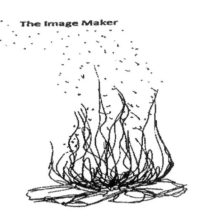

The Image Maker

We are refined by fire;
that is the medium You choose
to use to make us into Your image.

I am changed into Your image –
though I am tired. I sense
Your presence all around me.

I am moved within me
to reach for Your hand.
I am moved to
draw from Your strength
once again.

Draw me nearer,
nearer precious Lord
to the place where I belong.

The Building Foundation

It says that we build,
but someone else laid the foundation.
Unless the LORD builds the house, they labor in vain.
We are His workmanship, not the other way around.

What God desires to build in us is something

that you or I do not have within us to build.
What God builds is eternal. What we build
is only here for a short time - unless it's built
on something
that God did first.

"He who BEGAN a good work IN YOU..."

In contrast,
the building foundation of
our good works are as filthy rags!
And our filthy rags will stay here, on earth.

But whatever's done
in His name, that which
God desires to build inside of us,
THAT is eternal.

Fashion That

We don't fashion our God; how *we* want on bricks of clay.
We allow Him to fashion us into His image each day.

And whatever the King has built will stand and endure.
We will look differently than previous, then we did before.

But when we went out and started to fight
in our own strength, and in our own might,

the enemy drew us away and came to camp,
our fortified city he went back and made it a swamp.

We didn't have the goods to do the fighting... otherwise
Jesus wouldn't have died.
It wasn't our fight in the first place. *We* are the treasure.
The enemy lied.

A Marrieds' Joke

People say
That they want a formula
On 'how to Love God."

Can you IMAGINE
If you said to your spouse,
"I want to ask someone else
For a formula
On how to love *you* more."

Oh yeah,
That would go over well.

The Worst of Times

The loss of time is what hits me most.
Our physical bodies, our minds cry out,
"Everything I try takes a million years,
and everything I touch and start to do
gets blocked."

Our prayers and quiet times corporately
and individually are interrupted.
I know I must listen to my body – and I will.
I will get more accomplished if I listen.

Please, God, it doesn't even feel like I will
make it to 43. But You promised something,
and I believe in Your promise.

Created Equal

If we are really "in Christ,"
we are given front row seats
at what He is doing.

Knowing God's ways
We envelope one another
day after day.

Why did we see such a need
To capture one another?
Your life against mine.

Plow the field, mark the land.
Push the sun; I know
it will get hotter.

But I'm still standing.
Behold these truths to be self-evident,
That all men are created equal.

Endowed by their Creator
With certain unalienable rights.
Written near the time of 1776.

Battered and bruised, but
Still standing.
A long line, *time* worn.
The pursuit of happiness only runs
In life and liberty, we're satisfied.

What *time* zone?
He never slumbers or sleeps.
Forgive us our debts.
You have a long trail
Left to reason.

A Leaders Prayer II

God, I should decide if 'this' – my life,
my mission, etc. - is going to be about me
or if it is about You. If it is about You,
then I should relax and not worry.
I will make a mistake or two.

I can stay in the middle of my circumstance,
Or learn to wait on the Lord instead.
I may still choose to live in fear or worry,
and try to manipulate all sorts of situations.

Or I can rest. I choose to rest; watch what You
do in this situation. I said an unkind thing to someone today.
I will reap the consequences.
Will it ruin me forever? If it is about me, yes. BUT GOD.

I pray that I will learn from this situation.
Please change me; make me again.
And change my heart so that
I will bring glory to You once more.

Shortcomings

"These things I have spoken to you,
That in Me you may have peace.
In the world, you will have tribulation;
But be of good cheer,
I have overcome the world." (John 16:33)

God, I need You today. I sense
A certain hope for today, but the other side
of me is reluctant – to go out, to venture
past these walls.

God, give me the grace to accomplish
that which You have called me to do today. I
want to shine Your light, but I see
my frailties and my shortcomings.

The thing I want to do I don't do, and
the thing I dread I do. Who can save me
from this dead body? Praise be to God who
has given me Jesus. (Romans 7:13 – 8:11)

What's To Be Done

What do you do with what God gives you?
Do you just go through the words that are
said to you; look just once and then forget?

Or do you hear the Word, written down
and then forget the words?

The only way to get the full effect of what
God is saying
Is to take the words back out, over and over.
And bring them before the Lord who gave them.

Pray them back to God. Let Him hear your words again.
That way you are rehearsing what God has said to you.

Don't let the word be stolen away. Keep it fresh
in your mind and in your heart, even on your tongue.

Thanksgiving

Thanksgiving Day. Let Your will be done, God,
so that all may see Your glory. Let there come
a rise in understanding of what You want to do
in the earth.

Your will be done. Let us keep a spirit of
thankfulness – all throughout the day
and on into the holiday SEASON ahead
so that we might focus on what is important –

In life, in love, and not just what makes us happy
all the time....

The Spirit

Like a rain in the summer
on a beach of sand.
Like mid winter's slumber
from the snow that falls to the sand.
We are waiting on Your Spirit,
we are calling on Your grace,

to free us, free us, free us,
to see what You want
on the earth today.

Look Ahead

Go to the well; make God the center.
If you can't see what's in front of you, then
look ahead. Look at what God has already said.

He's done it for you, and look ahead.

His life was given on a cross
Wot that you could be free. He gave it all
So that your life could be changed.

Do you ever wonder why
God made you and why He allows
So much suffering? I'm not sure there's
An answer there, but I know
That He wants you to look ahead.

Look ahead at the wonderful things
That God has prepared for all those
who believe in Him. Look ahead
to what God's got in store.

He said He goes to prepare a place for us.
You know, if it wasn't true, He wouldn't have
Said it. He did once say, "I Am, the way, the
Truth, and the life."

Fence Sitter: a loving way to address a person
who makes a habit of stopping and looking
around instead of spending time with Him.
Instead of just taking Him at His word.

Christ died. Look ahead to what He has prepared
for all those who believe. It's the truth,
otherwise He wouldn't have said it.

A Veneer

Veneer: something put
on top of something else.
Or something put on top
of what's actually there.

If God doesn't build the house,
then it's just a veneer;
merely an outer shell.
Truly.

We cannot change ourselves.
All we can do
is give ourselves
a really good-looking veneer.

Someone may see your life and say,
"God has done so much in your life!"
And they will be encouraged.
We will be the only ones who will know
If it is real or just a veneer.

Batting a Thousand

Jesus said, "I have not lost one
that the Father has given me."
That's pretty good.
It is safe to put
our trust in Him.

Jesus has a perfect 'record.'
He isn't just batting a thousand.
This journey is longer than I thought.

Cyprus wash will still be here,
But this is a race, and I will get up and run.

What was done for the Lord will endure
Through all generations.
Living the life within the lines.
The rest is batting a thousand.

The Truth

Tell the Truth.

When the enemy
throws something 'in your face.'
When he says that you will never amount
to anything, don't go along with him,
even one more inch.

Tell the Truth.

When you are tempted to quit
and you feel pushed over the edge,
don't give in;
and tell yourself the Truth.

When life is too much to bear,
and your friends have walked away,
and you feel everyone around is laughing
don't listen to that lie.
Tell yourself the Truth.

We live in an age
when it is much easier to 'follow the crowd'
and listen to what *they* have to say.
They 'make up the story'
of our lives sometimes. It is much easier to hear than to

dig in and find out what He said about us.

The Truth, the Living Word.
The inherent voice of God at our fingertips!
There for all to see. Yet we miss the opportunity
to live with this living Word *inside* our lives.

And sometimes, instead, we listen to those people
who don't have any real knowledge of what
we are going through on the *inside*.
They just see what we are on the outside.
And they miss the story.

Oh God, the Truth, dwells in me.

A Protest

We say that we are for freedom,
yet we've gone SO FAR
from what freedom is all about.
This one area alone makes me want to picket.

The Question

Do you still have your song from Sunday?
Is the song that was instilled in you Sunday
still in your heart?

Does that song you sing during the week
reflect that 'just married' quality?

"A Little Encouragement Here"

A little encouragement here!
Thoughts and feelings, like everything around me has been
under construction, that Your presence has been
far from me, and I was falling into disrepair.

But You have a plan for everything
and the silent times are Yours as well.
The events of today are a show of
Your sovereignty in not forgetting me.

I believe that I have tried to have my ideas
and they have not gone anywhere. But today
I have hope that I should keep trying.

The enemy was like a predator, ready to
pounce on its prey. When I heard a rustling sound,
he turned and I heard myself saying, "I saw you defeated;
you have no business here." And then he was gone.

The Bible: What It is Not

So, if I use the word 'Bible,'
There are many thoughts
that come to mind.
"The first thing I think of
is God being angry."
But God is the Creator. Is He
angry with Himself?

"And hell and fire."
Yes, He created that too.

"I know: You're all going to burn."
That's in the Bible,
but that's attitude, somehow
dressed up in a suit.

"And someone
handing out candy."
I think that's what
we call church.

"And having games
and rides and all that."
Social gospel, yes,
but none of that's Bible.

None of it. That is
just religion.
You told me what the Bible is not.

The Un-Changeables

God, unless You change me I will not be changed.
That is a two-fold prayer; it's a double-edged sword.
Whatever God has built into our life,
That will stand forever.
It is unchangeable: God's word; those things
which He has built inside of you. So "God, unless You change me
I will not be moved." That is a promise from God.

When I say, "unless you change me,"
it means that heaven and earth will pass away,
but what God has done will never pass away.

Then, the other side of that same prayer –
"God, unless You change me
I will not be changed – that
I cannot be the one moving myself.

That is the desire of heaven; that you would be
made into His image. And that which God does in you
will never be moved.

The way we've always thought about,
that's the traditional way; that I will not
'be' changed, unless You change me.

It can 'be' frustrating. Others want you to 'be,'
And you want 'to be' changed, but you just
cannot change or mold yourself. What are you to do?

It can also be that *You*, God, have all things
in Your hands, and that those things
which You will implement on the earth will never be moved.

And what is inside of me,
and what You have put in my life
from Your word, everything that
goes in from You, that we pray and say,
"Father, change me. That I would be
changed into Your image." Those things
will stand forever. Those things which
God is the One who nailed it in,
and put it in our lives. It will not be moved.

God is faithful. If we put our faith in Him,
those things which He has put inside of us
will not change. There is an impossibility
because we are tied to – we are living with –
a Living God. And that God will change us.

And that change which He makes
cannot be revoked: by someone else,
or by anything, if we have our eyes
fixed on God. We have our hope in Him.

Everything that comes against us – whether
spiritual or inner fears – cannot prosper.
We are no longer the one trying to
hold it back in our own strength.

We *know* that we have just a little strength.
And the God that we serve has ALL strength.
He is faithful, the One who has promised it.
He will not allow our foot to stumble.

As we walk toward Him, though we may be
in the midst of a difficult situation, and
it looks the darkest. We learn that He is the
Immutable; the unchangeable God!

Because of what He does inside of us, we can say,
"Father, unless You change me, I WILL NOT be changed."
We can see His love continuously
because of what He has done.

God, unless You change me, I will not be changed.
I will not be moved. And though heaven and earth
pass away, Your word which You have built
will never pass away.

The Contrast of Change

A lot of times
we want to prepare ourselves.
But God wants to prepare *us*

for eternity.

We see the natural light, the physical,
and sometimes we are short-sighted.
If we put our hand to something.
Then it is just flesh. And it says that
flesh works itself out in the flesh.
But that which God does
abides forever.

When we abide, are changed by the Living God,
then the change is Spirit.
If we do the changing,
that means that we should be able
to boast
about something we had done.
Yet it says that
'salvation comes in no other Name.'
So, there's no room for boasting.

If it is all about God -
and what He has done -
then the enemy of our souls
has *nothing* to hold on to
and condemn us with;
if all that is inside of us is done
by the Living God.

It is no longer
I who live,
but Christ
lives in me.

So that which is done in us,
Is done by the One, True, Living God.
So when we are asked, "What is

the hope that lies within you?"
Then we will have a clear answer
because it's based on faith,
and not on works.
"That which is flesh is flesh.
And that which is Spirit
Is spirit."

The change:
Total domination over my heart, soul,
mind, and strength.

The Hard Line

Sometimes it just takes me knowing
that others are praying for me;
that others have prayed for me.

The hard line:
Asking, God, what else is there
besides suicide and bumping ourselves?

Jesus went through these feelings,
though without caving into sin.

He who knew no sin, became sin,
so that we might become
the righteousness of God in Him.

He made Him who knew no sin
To become sin on our behalf!
So that our generation – from Adam
to the end - would be
able to choose.

Intellectual Property

We usually hear the term 'Intellectual Property'
When someone has stolen 'identity" or 'property'
On the internet. But what about power
Over another person?

We think that our thoughts and actions -
Whether a person is present or not -
Have no bearing on that person;
That it can't hurt them to talk 'behind
Their back.'

But what you *say* and *think* is called
Intellectual Property: that which you think.

In other words, some other countries have a much better view
Of this stuff than we do. People in Korea
Have taken centuries to work on this aspect of their lives.

They have learned by experience
That what you say and do, and how we treat one another
In our mind, can be as much killing
As taking out a knife and 'finishing the job.'

But God said, in the second Person in the Trinity,
"If you say to your neighbor, 'Raca,'
[which means 'fool,'] you have killed that person
In your heart. (The heart is desperately wicked,
Who can know it.)

We do not have the power to do right. Not even
The sweetest, most intelligent and kind person
Has the power to do good all the time.
That's why we need a Savior.

God of Heaven

There is
in Beijing
   one temple called the Heavenly Temple.
(Nehemiah 1:4) "And it came to pass,
   when I heard these words, and mourned certain days;
and I fasted and prayed before the God of heaven."

   Only the God of heaven can inhabit
the praises of those that seek Him, the God of Heaven.
   The Heavenly Temple is made
to the specs of Solomon's Temple; David's.

   (Song of Solomon 2:16-17) "My beloved
is mine, and I am his: He feeds his flock among the lilies.
   Until the day be cool, and the shadows flee away,
turn, and be like a roe or a young hart upon the mountains of Bether."

(Matthew 6:9-11) "Our Father, ..."

The Opposites

Faith and fear. Some see faith as an outgrowth of going through
   some fearful situations.
But faith and fear
   are really opposites. One stands and sees a situation and is
   paralyzed at the thought of walking
through 'that.'
   If we face in the direction of 'faith,' "this chair is not going to
   break when we sit down on it" – then
We cannot *see* fear; it is behind us.

But if we are facing fear, we will fall down as soon as our feet touch
the bottom of the creek bed;
   The water is rushing around our feet
So fast that we cannot stand against the current. We *will* fall.
   Face one direction – faith or fear - and you will always follow that
   path.

The Aroma Gospel

To the one
   I'm like the smell of death. (I have an aroma about me.)
But to the other,
   It is 'the smell of life.'

The gospel should be sweet smelling; a sacrifice, acceptable to God.
   America has need for Christ.
Jesus 'married' grace and truth; He never sacrificed one for the other.

Romans 6:14 is written
   To people that have received the gospel,
And want to live by God's laws. Behavior follows
   the surrendering. If we surrender to the flesh,
then we look like the flesh. It's so easy to live there: works.

   But Law is outside law, if written on the heart
and becomes grace. John 8:32, you will *know* (gnosco) the truth
   and the truth will make you free; the true aroma of the gospel.
Jesus is grace; a Person.

With One Play to Run

Picture this: The Holy Spirit, The Coach.
How ridiculous! But I'd like to say the Coach is
the Holy Spirit: ever present, and continually
telling us which 'plays' to Run. And remember:
on a team playing without opposition is
against the rules.

Everyone's ready to start the field, then
the opposition comes out: Big team; well formed
and well practiced. And the team that was ready
begins to sit down and have lunch. Or they
begin to form little groups, which begin to look at
faults of their own teammates. How ridiculous does that sound!
Getting out to the field and all that time spent getting ready...

And all that time there is a Great Crowd gathered
to witness the game. We need to determine once and for all,
whose team we are on;
we need to be a part
of the team, not some
faction on 'the outside
looking in.'

And we should *always* be
looking at our teammates;
how we can make the team
even stronger. As we participate in the struggle,
believe it or not, it's the struggle that makes us
stronger; it's the struggle that makes us even closer
as a team.

And it's the struggle that 'cleans' us. You don't have to
Do or be anything before you join in the team; it's just

Imperative that you Run in the game.
If we are on the Divine Triune Creator's team –
and He being the owner of the club – has already
given us The 'Book.' And He wins.

Remember: The little or much that you participate
on 'the field' is more than the person who stands
on the sidelines and yells at his teammates.
We already have the Holy Spirit.

My Under Wear

I'm still working on my 'under wear' manners. What I mean is,
    that I can see how I am
when nobody's looking. And sometimes
    I get 'all tied up.'
So, who I am
    When nobody's looking
Is who I am. Really.

The Dark Side

I had my moment in the sun.
I wasn't a believer, but I went to church.
A girl had 'done me wrong,' and I was
going to 'teach her a lesson.'

But what I learned from that situation was

that that made me very popular; everyone
knew my name. I was 'the talk of the town.'
I had my moment in the sun.

I never talked with that girl again.
And in some ways my 'time in the sun' felt good.
I had people's attention. And in some ways…
I never want to see the sun again.

A Journal

So, here we are again, Lord. I fall
on Your mercies that are new every morning.

A new journal, Lord God;
we have been at this
for quite some time:
writing a journal.
I started at the age of 16,
but I have lost most of the journals I've written.

Yet the writing itself is what helped me:
Through years of deep healing;
Through wounds,
Through those first years of hearing You speak;
learning to talk to You
by getting my feelings down on paper.

Learned Obedience

Today. The washer is running in the background.
I'm sitting with a sore body
and find myself taking two different antibiotics.

I'm in pain and want to 'squeeze' the sickness out of
my body but can't.

"And Jesus learned obedience from the things
that He suffered." "No servant is above his master."
Does that mean that Jesus was imperfect? That
He lacked something and the obedience was
meant for His good?

Let light shine out of darkness. In the
dark places, You are there. In the midst
of pain, You are there as well.
Let Your kingdom come. More of You, Lord.

Not flowery words, but
Words that will heal, and clarify, and make clean.
You have promised that if we watch over Your stuff,
that You will watch over our stuff. I think I like that exchange.

Waiting Like a Lover

God, You wait
for Your servants,
and give
Grace to the humble.

You give good gifts
to those that
have seen Your face in
the land of the living.

And we
Will rejoice
in what You've done.

By Just One Word

By just a word You created the earth
And all that's in it.

By one word You had armies of very few men
Overpower their enemies.

By the breath of Your mouth
You brought back people to life.

And by just one word You
Raised Yourself from the dead.

I do believe, God of Heaven and Earth;
Help my unbelief.
I walk as one who has seen great injustice
And lived through it to tell about Your power.

I've seen the wrong turned to right. Please,
Help me believe You now.

Printed in the United States
By Bookmasters